James Anthony Froude

Two Lectures on South Africa,

Delivered before the Philosophical Institute, Edinburgh, Jan. 6 and 9, 1880

James Anthony Froude

Two Lectures on South Africa,
Delivered before the Philosophical Institute, Edinburgh, Jan. 6 and 9, 1880

ISBN/EAN: 9783744755832

Printed in Europe, USA, Canada, Australia, Japan

Cover: Foto ©Thomas Meinert / pixelio.de

More available books at **www.hansebooks.com**

TWO LECTURES

ON

SOUTH AFRICA

DELIVERED BEFORE THE PHILOSOPHICAL INSTITUTE

EDINBURGH, JAN. 6 & 9, 1880

BY

JAMES ANTHONY FROUDE, M.A.

LONDON

LONGMANS, GREEN, AND CO.

1880

SOUTH AFRICA.

—◦◦⦂◦⦂◦◦—

LECTURE I.

LADIES AND GENTLEMEN,—An invitation to lecture
before the Philosophical Institution at Edinburgh
is a high compliment, but also an embarrassing
one. You have been addressed, and will be addressed during this session, by many able speakers
on weighty matters, scientific or literary. It has
been difficult for me to select a subject on which I
have anything to say which can deserve a place in
so distinguished a series. I turned over in my
mind various periods of Scotch history, hoping to
find something which might answer the purpose.
I thought at one time I would make a lecture out
of the Scotch Statute-book. There is pleasant read-
ing in that book, only it is a little dry. Old statutes
are like the ivory carvings which are found in
Egyptian and Assyrian tombs. They have lost
their gelatine : we have to put the human life and
juice into them again ; and this is rather work for

B

the laboratory than the lecture-room. And, besides, Scotch laws are rather dangerous ground for an un-professional stranger like myself to venture upon, especially before a Scotch audience. I might find myself caught in a steel trap before I was clear of the Regiam Majestatem.

I could not run this risk. I decided after some reflection that for once I would leave the history of the past, and turn to a question of present interest and the present time. I may make mistakes in talking about it, but if I do there is no danger of your detect-ing me. I wish there was. For the South African question is a very knotty one indeed, and the knots can only be untied when the British people will please to pay attention to it. We can hardly say that it is of no importance to us. We have just been killing about twenty thousand people in South Africa—people who had done us no harm ; we only feared that perhaps they might do us harm. We have annexed a country as large as France, which belonged to Dutchmen. Dutchmen do not like to have their independence taken from them any more than we do, and nobody exactly knows why we did it. I believe that in our hearts we are sorry now that we annexed it at all, and would be glad to get rid of it again, if we only knew how to get rid of it without seeming ridiculous to the rest of the world.

We have a little bill still to pay for these amusements. When Parliament meets, the Chancellor of the Exchequer will tell us how many millions he wants from us. I do not know what the sum will be—we may be sure it will be larger than his estimate, because I never knew an instance where money spent in wars did not prove larger than the estimate. Some one, I suppose, will then ask what the war was about, and what good has come of it. The good will prove to be about as much as there is in a noble lord's pheasant battue—or perhaps less than that—for the pheasants can at least be eaten. Everybody will be sorry ; we shall make the best resolutions ; the newspapers will assure us that it is the last time; no more English armies will be sent to South Africa ; the colonists must fight their own battles for the future. So newspapers and politicians said five-and-twenty years ago, so they repeated seven years ago ; yet here we are just emerging from the worst affair that we ever were engaged in there. Our 'shalls' and 'musts' are as ineffectual as the 'shalls' and 'musts' of children. As sure as the leaves come when summer comes, fresh troubles of the same kind will continue to return upon us, unless we—the British people—set ourselves to understand how they are brought about. The problem is a complicated one. The newspapers say that we have only to do as we did in New Zealand, and withdraw our troops. I think I can show you that no

such royal road is open for us to escape by. You
will not at any rate consider an hour or two thrown
away if I use them to make the situation clear to
you. It so happens that a few circumstances con-
nected with the present state of things can be better
explained by me than by anyone, for I was per-
sonally concerned in them. I have never yet had
an opportunity of describing what took me to South
Africa, or how I came to be mixed up with the in-
tricacies of Colonial politics. As long as there was
a hope that the country would settle down into any
kind of order, I preferred to say as little as I could
help about it. The country has not settled down.
It is not in the way of settling; we may win vic-
tories, but they only make the clouds thicken ; and
clouds in South Africa generally break in thunder-
storms, and peculiarly vicious ones.

What I shall have to say has nothing to do with
party politics. I know your rule here ; and if you
had no such rule, nothing could be more misleading
than to treat the troubles which have arisen at the
Cape of Good Hope as the results of a Liberal policy
or of a Conservative policy. Neither are Liberals
specially to blame nor Conservatives ; we are merely
reaping the harvest now of seventy years of misman-
agement. Tory statesmen and Whig statesmen have
alike borne their part in it, and we cannot throw
stones at one another. The mistakes of both have

risen from the simplest of causes. They have been attempting to govern a country six thousand miles off, of which they did not know anything, and took no pains to learn anything ; and yet (we ought not, perhaps, to wonder at it) they never suspected their own ignorance. They have had certain fixed ideas, not always consistent, that the Dutch were a very wicked people ; that the natives were innocent and harmless, or would be if the Dutch would let them alone.

Under the impression of these ideas they have attempted alternately to coerce the Dutch or to leave them to govern themselves; to protect the natives or make war upon them, and annex their territories. At one time we have insisted that the South Africans shall act as we please. Then we have told them to do as they please and to trouble us with their affairs no further. The story of our rule at the Cape is a story of vacillation varied with tyranny, which can be paralleled only in the history of our rule in Ireland. We say of our treatment of Ireland that if we had lived in the days of our fathers we would not have been partakers of their evil deeds. I am afraid that, like the Jews, we are showing ourselves our fathers' sons, and are treading in their steps and imitating their example with the most filial devoutness.

Therefore I am not going to quarrel especially with

anything which this Government has done or the late Government or any Government. I am going simply to tell you what the state of South Africa was when I was there, why I went out, what persons I saw, what they said to me, and what came of it. You will then, I think, be at least able to understand how all these wonderful wars and annexations have been brought about, and why they have not brought South Africa a step nearer to quiet and content.

I will begin with the briefest possible account of these South African settlements, what they are and how they came into our possession.

We speak of South Africa as an English colony. It is not a colony. It is a conquered country, of which we took possession for our own purposes against the wish of its proper owners. English colonists have since settled there : but South Africa is Dutch. The laws are Dutch, the language, over the greater part of it, is Dutch. The Dutch occupied it more than two hundred years ago. They subdued the Hottentots, they destroyed the wild beasts. They built farmhouses and towns. They planted trees and vineyards. Forests of oak and pine introduced from Holland still speak for their industry. I have myself been a guest in Dutch houses in the interior which were built far back in the last century. English colonists go to South Africa to make money, and come back with it. To the Dutch settlers it is still a home, the only home they have. There they planted themselves, there they took root, and raised their families. There they mean to stay. It is their country. They feel for it as you do for Scotland or the French for France. They look on us as intruders. They hope to have it again one day for themselves, and the Dutch are a tough, stubborn, independent people, as the Spaniards and Austrians found to their cost when they tried to master them in Europe.

How, then, did we come by South Africa ? After the French revolution the armies of the Convention overran Holland. It became for a time a French province, and the Dutch colonies, it was feared, would share the misfortunes of the mother-country. The Cape was on the high road to India. The Cape was then as important to England as the Suez Canal is now. At the extreme point of the African continent there is a land-locked bay : it is the one harbour where a naval arsenal can be made for several thousand miles. An enemy in possession of Simon's Bay could intercept the entire ocean traffic between Europe and the East. For this reason we took it. For this reason we are obliged to keep it. The Suez Canal may be blocked any day, and we may be driven back on the old route.

We occupied the Cape in 1795. The party in Holland who were opposed to France approved. The

Cape colonists made slight resistance. It was understood that we went there only as a garrison, and that on the peace it would be restored. At the Peace of Amiens it was in fact restored; but war broke out again immediately, and we went back. This time the colonists did not admit us so quietly. They armed; they fought gallantly for their liberties; they were defeated, and they submitted a second time. We said that we should go away again when the war was finally over. It would have been better, I think, both for us and for South Africa if we had gone away. A high-spirited population never willingly submits to be ruled by strangers. The conqueror forgets. The conquered does not forget, and nourishes hopes which spring again when opportunity offers. The English, however, when in possession of places which they find convenient, are apt to stay there. We had got hold of the Cape; we wished to keep our hold, and at the Congress of Vienna it was arranged as we desired. The Dutch colonists were not consulted.

The English nation is the most conscientious in the world in judging the faults of its neighbours. If France, or Germany, or Russia, annexes territories belonging to other people we cannot express our disapprobation too strongly. We ourselves have swallowed more territory than all the other nations put together; but we only do it for the benefit of

mankind. It may have been politic to retain the
Cape. Doubtless strong reasons might be urged for
it, but as certainly it was retained against the wishes
of its owners. It would have been prudent therefore
if we had considered the feelings of these owners,
and had exerted ourselves to reconcile them to the
change.

I suppose we regard the liberty of being British
subjects as so great a blessing in itself that no other
liberty is worth talking about in comparison. The
Cape Dutch unfortunately did not properly appreciate
their privilege. When it was known that we were
not going away, a few hot-spirited young colonists
rebelled. They were soon crushed. We sympathise
generally with insurgents in other countries. Insurrection against ourselves we treat as if it was
something peculiarly wicked. The rebel leaders
were hanged, and the martyrs of Slaughter Neck are
remembered in Dutch households in South Africa
much as your own Wallace is remembered here. The
Dutch farmers, however (Boers we call them : it simply
means farmers), are a practical people. Their thoughts
are chiefly taken up with their families and properties,
and by this time they would have forgotten their
martyrs if we had not taken care to ensure that they
should recollect them ; but from that time dates a
feeling of irritation against the Boers in the English
governing classes, which has shown itself whenever

opportunity has offered, and the sore has been so aggravated and irritated and kept open, that I know not now how it can be cured.

In 1820 a few thousand English and Scots were planted in the eastern part of the colony. A certain number of Dutch had already settled there; but there was room for both. They and the new-comers soon became good friends. They had a common enemy in the Kafir. They suffered together from his incursions over the Fish River. They fought on each other's side, and protected and sheltered each other's families. Very soon they would have become one people. But a new source of bitterness was now opened. The English nation had suddenly become alive to the enormity of slavery. No people had been more active in propagating slavery than we had been. As our crimes were great, so was our repentance; and we expected our colonists, whose properties were at stake, to be converted at the same moment that we were. All over the empire the slaves were to be set at liberty, and we voted twenty millions in compensation to the owners of them. It was a right and necessary thing to do; we admired our own virtue perhaps a little too much; but that may be forgiven. The South African Dutch were among the sinners. Slavery with them, however, was not the horrible thing which it had been in the West Indies. They had no cane plantations or cotton-fields. Their slaves were household servants, much like what serfs used to be in England. They lived under their master's roof, or in houses on his estate, and were part of his family. The evidence showed that of all the slaves who were to be set free there were none who had less to complain of than those of the Dutch farmers at the Cape. No owner who was called on to part with his property had a fairer right to his share in the twenty millions. The Dutch farmer did not get his share. The valuation was first, I think, reduced by one-half. Then, for some reason known to themselves, the Government refused to send the money out. The claim, such as it was, could only be met in London. The farmers, not being able to go to London, had to negotiate with agents, at a further loss of twenty per cent., and the end of it was that a great many of them refused to receive the miserable sum which was allotted to them, and it remains to this day undemanded. The slaves themselves showed so little appreciation of what was done for them that they generally stayed with their masters' families. I have myself been waited on in patriarchal Dutch houses by ancient white-haired negroes, the survivors of the old days. The estates are still cultivated by the sons and grandsons of the field hands, who continue to live at the old spots in cottages of their own, and work for wages from the masters' descendants. This is the present relation between the Dutch Boers and the representatives of their old bondmen in the western part of the Cape Colony. We may draw from it what inferences we please.

Unjust treatment in the slavery matter did not improve their relations with the Colonial Office. Another measure provoked them still more. The Dutch nowhere allow vagrancy in their colonies. Java is a Dutch colony. When we made over Java to Holland, the population of it was nine millions; it is now eighteen millions. You never hear of famine in Java ; you hear no complaints. The exports increase ; the people increase and multiply. Java— I wish I could say as much of any colony of ours— pays a revenue to the mother-country. I asked a Dutch gentleman once to explain all this to me. I inquired if there was slavery in Java. 'Oh,' he said, ' God forbid that a Christian people should be so wicked as to hold slaves. They all work without that.' How was it possible? I inquired, were they never idle? ' Oh,' he said, ' no one is allowed to be idle.'

This meant, of course, that in Java every man is obliged to earn his living. The people are tied to their respective districts, and are made to maintain themselves and their families. It was the law in England once; it was the law all over Europe down to these latter days of liberty and enlightenment.

Liberty to be idle may be an excellent thing in the perfect state at which we have now arrived, but it is not always suitable in lower degrees of civilisation.

What the Holland Dutch do now in Java, the Cape Dutch had done for the Hottentots seventy years ago. They were restrained from vagrancy; they were forced to live in a settled home and cultivate the ground. In the first enthusiasm for emancipation a labour law was regarded as another form of slavery. The Hottentots were released; they were allowed to go where they pleased; they drank, they stole; the farmers were ruined for want of workmen. To the Hottentots themselves freedom was no unmixed blessing. There were then 150,000 of them; there are now, I think, about 20,000, if so many. The rest have perished by drink and disease.

In these and other ways too many to mention, the English Government came into collision with its unwilling subjects. The English Government thought the Boers perverse and good for nothing. The Boers, who had hated the English occupation from the first, resolved to recover their liberty, and in 1836 many thousands of them broke up from their homes, packed their household goods, their family Bibles, and their rifles, into their ox-waggons, and streamed away into the interior, across the Orange

River. Their adventures will form an epic poem, if a man of genius ever rises to write such a thing. Some of the native tribes were friendly to them, some were hostile. They fought battles, they made treaties. At length they created two new States, now known as the Orange Free State and the Transvaal: vast, open, pastoral countries, where they settled down and throve. They were enterprising. They wanted access to the sea for their wool trade. A party of them crossed the Drachenberg Mountains and went down into Natal, which then belonged to Dingaan, the grandfather of the much talked-of Cetewayo. Peter Retief, the leader of this detachment, was like an old Israelite of the days of the Judges, a pious, good, true man, and as brave as a lion. Natal was then a desert : the Zulus had destroyed its old inhabitants. They professed to be willing to allow Retief to occupy it. The terms were arranged. He went unarmed with sixty companions to the Zulu chief to ratify the treaty. They were all murdered ; their camp was attacked ; their women and children were murdered also. The Zulu triumph was short. Another Dutch force came down, reinforced from the colony; Dingaan was killed. Natal became a third free Dutch State. The Boers built Maritzburg, the present capital, and they had a port of their own at Durban.

Thus matters stood in 1840. The Dutch were

now in possession of a new country, stretching down to the sea, and completely shielding the colony from contact with the interior tribes, especially from the dangerous Zulus. Our whole frontier was secured. The Kafirs in the mountains between Natal and the eastern province were cut off from all communication with the rest of their kindred, and with the Dutch on one side and us on the other would soon have ceased to give trouble. They might have remained in harmless independence. The English Government, it might have been expected, would have welcomed an arrangement which relieved it of its discontented subjects and saved it all further expense and trouble. Happy we should be if we could now replace South Africa in the position into which it had then adjusted itself. If the Colonial Office was asked at this moment to dispose the European settlers in that country in the position most convenient to ourselves, it would be this very one which had then been spontaneously created.

Reason and good sense, however, generally come too late in human affairs. We act in passion and prejudice ; we reflect when it is too late. Downing Street was then possessed with a spirit of philanthropy. Of true and wise philanthropy there is never too much in this world ; of emotional philanthropy we may easily have too much. It was then our special mission to protect the native races. To the native races we attributed every conceivable virtue ; to the Boers every imaginable fault. Our peace of mind requires us to think ill of those we have injured. It was decided that these Boer emigrants could not shake off their allegiance. Where they went we must follow, and maintain our authority over them. Natal was taken first, as being accessible from the sea. The Boers fought for it, but they were beaten back over the mountains, and Natal became English. It has not been a very valuable possession to us. Now, after forty years of occupation, there are but 20,000 Europeans there, and of these only half are of British birth. The rest are still Dutch, who had property which they could not abandon. The country is almost wholly uncultivated. Multitudes of natives have flocked into it. They prefer idleness to work. The Government does not insist on their doing any work. They live upon their cattle and their Indian corn, which their women raise for them. Divided from Natal only by the Tugela River are our late foes, the Zulus, of whose fighting qualities we know more than we could wish. We chose to take Natal. It is entirely useless to us ; yet we cannot get rid of it; and there we stand with the Zulus for neighbours, backed by the infinite population of Africa which lies behind them.

After Natal came the Orange River territory.

Thither also it was thought necessary to follow up the unfortunate Boers. Again there was a battle; again many lives were thrown away. We gained fresh dominions, which again were valueless to us, and another item was added to the list of wrongs which the South African Dutch record against us as faithfully as an Irishman records the penal laws.

Wherever we went on this wild Boer hunt, trouble followed us like a shadow. We had crossed the Orange River to protect the native tribes. They did not want our protection, and we fell into wars with them. The Basutos fought well, and we did not always come off with credit. We found our benevolence at once expensive and ineffectual. Reflection came at last, and Downing Street changed its policy. We discovered, what we ought to have discovered before, that an independent Dutch State beyond the Orange River covered our frontier and saved us money and responsibility. We acknowledged our mistake; we drew back, and in 1851 and 1852, in two separate conventions, we left the Dutch in possession of the Orange River territory and the Transvaal. We bound ourselves never more to interfere between them and the natives. The Orange River was to be our future boundary, which under no conditions were we ever more to pass. Natal, to our sorrow, we did not give back. Natal we chose to hold in the same spirit in which we ruined the manufactures of Ireland. The miserable resemblance of policy meets us at every turn. We did not wish these Dutch to be too prosperous, so we shut them out from the sea.

Leave these States however we did, and, as far as it went, it was the wisest step we ever took in that country. Seventeen years followed : the quietest which South Africa has known since we came into possession of it. The two Republics prospered beyond our expectation, and, I fear, beyond our wishes. We had promised to leave them alone entirely. We never did entirely leave them alone. The English colonists had objected to the arrangement from the first. They had vague ambitions of an English South African empire, and the Free States were in the way of it.

Reports of the Boers' cruelties found ready listeners at the Colonial Office. Rough things were of course done. Border farmers had their cattle stolen. The thieves were pursued to their villages, and there were often fights. Women and men go into battle together in those countries. When a village was destroyed, native children would be found whose fathers and mothers had been killed. The children would have died had they been left. The Boers took them away, and brought them up as servants. At times gross wrong may have been done in this way; at other times it may have been an act of humanity. Be that as it will, violence and lawlessness were inevitable among men cast loose to take care of themselves in so enormous an extent of country. But very soon, with a rapidity far beyond what their warmest friends looked for, a regular government was set up, with paid magistrates and a police. Thousands of miles of roads were opened; towns were built and churches; solid farmsteads rose, and lands were enclosed and planted. With due observance made for their circumstances their success was extraordinary. The Dutch in the old Cape colony almost forgot their anger at us in their pleasure at the prosperity of their kindred. Part of their race at least was free and happy. We on our part had no more native wars, and we hoped that we had heard the last of them.

Unluckily we did not know when we were well off. When we withdrew we left the Orange Free State a legacy in the shape of a quarrel with the Basutos, which, after smouldering for some years, burst out into a war. There were four years of fighting. At the end of these years the Dutch had beaten the Basutos, and intended to tie them up, that they might have no more trouble with them. It was one of those cases which had been foreseen when the independence was conceded. We had promised to take no part, but we had already half repented of our promise. Treaty or no treaty, we thought it impossible to leave the Boers to crush a tribe who had measured arms not unsuccessfully with ourselves. We took the Basutos under our protection, and robbed the Dutch of half the profit of their victory. It was a distinct breach of promise—our action was so manifestly unjust that it roused a natural indignation among the Dutch of the colony. To pacify them the convention of 1852 was renewed at Aliwal in 1869, and we again pledged ourselves, with all the solemnity of a formal engagement, to interfere no farther to the north of the Orange River.

This, you will observe, was in the year 1869. We are now on the edge of the events which have led to the present confusion.

In that same year, unfortunately (I say unfortunately, for though it filled South Africa with money, it tempted England into one of the most scandalous acts recorded in our history) there was discovered, in a corner of the country which since 1852 had been occupied and administered by the Free State magistrates, the most remarkable diamond mine which has yet been found. The mine had come as a Godsend to the poor Free State, exhausted as it was by the war. It would bring wealth, it would bring immigrants. It would give them a lift, which it was unworthy of us to envy them.

But now observe what followed. No State but England could be allowed to possess the finest diamond mine in the world. We had abandoned the Orange

River territory because we thought it was useless. The situation was altered altogether when it was found to contain unimagined wealth. I acquit the English authorities of doing anything which they consciously knew to be wrong. When Englishmen wish that a particular course shall be right, they are perfectly convinced that it is right. A case was got up—I cannot go into the history of it—to show that the land where the diamonds had been found did not belong to the Dutch at all, but belonged to a native chief. It was represented also that a large and lawless population would collect at the mine, and that the Dutch would be unable to keep order there. These things were pressed upon the Government at Home, and at once were taken into consideration by it.

One would have thought that, with the ink scarce dry on the treaty at Aliwal, the consideration need not have been a long one; we had pledged our word; surely we ought to have kept it. It might have been true that the republic would have proved unequal to keeping the peace; but it would have been time to act when disorder broke out; or if we repented of having let the Free State go, and wished to recover it, the English diggers at the mine would have brought it back to us constitutionally.

These arguments would perhaps have prevailed but for the inveterate prejudice against the Boers at the Colonial Office. The Colonial Secretary was, in fact, unwilling to move in the matter. But a political experiment was at that moment being carried out in the English Colonies. The English Government wished to be rid of its Colonial responsibilities. Constitutions, with power to manage their own affairs, had been granted to the Canadians and Australians. It had been decided to apply the same principle at the Cape. Many sensible people doubted whether responsible government, as it is called, would answer in South Africa. You may conquer a people and hold them subject, and govern them your own way. You cannot so easily conquer a people and tell them to govern themselves in a way which you will like. When a colony receives a Constitution, the troops are to be withdrawn, and it is understood that if it wishes to be independent it is at liberty to leave us. But we cannot withdraw the troops from Cape Town, and we cannot let South Africa be independent, because we must not part with the naval station. And, again, Natal was obviously unfit for responsible government; while it was inexpedient in a high degree to part with our control over the Cape Colony while we had possessions in the same country which could not be included under the same form of administration. The English Ministry was in too great a hurry. English Ministries often are in too great a hurry. They know that their time is short, and when they

begin a work they wish to finish it before they leave
office. Perhaps they thought that responsible
government would please the Cape Dutch, and reconcile them to English sovereignty. If this was
their motive, it was a pity they paid so little attention
to Dutch sentiment. They passed over the government of the Colony to the Cape Parliament, a large
majority of the members of it being returned by
Dutch constituencies. They chose that particular
moment to do what every Dutchman in South Africa
regarded as a most outrageous injury. I must do the
Ministry justice. They were deceived by false ac-
counts of the people's wishes. They never dreamt of
keeping the Diamond Fields as a possession of the
Crown. They meant it as a handsome present to the
Colony. With this view they set aside the treaty,
though it was but a short year old. They flung
away the old policy, which kept the Colony behind
the Orange River. They seized the mine and the
territory round it, excusing themselves by charging
the Orange Free State with having stolen it from
the native chief. Never was there such an illustration
of the story of the wolf and the lamb. In forming
their new province they cut into the Transvaal as
well as the Free State. The two States refused to
admit our right to plunder them, and the whole
district was thrown into anger and confusion. The
farmers did not know under what jurisdiction they

were living. English and Dutch officials came in daily collision. The Orange Free State published a protest, and demanded the arbitration of some foreign Power.

The effect was even worse in the Cape Colony itself. The Parliament at Cape Town had sanctioned the annexation by a small minority. But the constituencies made the Parliament change its note. The Dutch took the injury to their kindred as an injury to themselves, and it was found that no Ministry could stand which proposed to take charge of the Diamond Fields.

Thus at the moment when we were trying to escape our South African responsibilities, we found ourselves saddled with a new province in the heart of the country, up beyond the Orange River, where we had promised never to go, and execrated by the very people whom we had most desired to please.

All Cabinets make mistakes, and we may easily be too hard on them. The appropriation of the mine was well intended, no doubt; but the laws of nature do not care about intentions. Water will run down-hill if we make an opening for it, although we had meant it to run the other way. We chose to throw away our old prudent policy; we broke faith, and broken faith never leads to good. Every misfortune which has fallen upon the country since—Kafir

wars, Zulu wars, the annexation of the Transvaal,
and the confusion which now prevails—are distinctly
traceable to this one unfortunate act.

If the Free States had stood alone they might
have submitted ; but they were assured of the
support of the Colony—and the Colony had now
a government of its own. The old dogged anti-
English feeling was raised in all its bitterness. The
Boer responds more readily than most men to kindness and justice ; if you try to drive him, there is no
mule in either hemisphere more stubborn.

Let us put ourselves in his position for a moment.
In our opinion it is a high privilege to be a British
subject ; other nations do not look upon it in the
same light. When our Edward annexed Scotland,
he thought that he was conferring on Scotland a
very high distinction. You yourselves took another
view of the matter. People will be blind in these
things.

The President of the Orange Free State refused
to recognise the Governor whom we set up at the
Diamond Fields, and denied constantly that he had
any business to be there. An arbitration was tried
with the Transvaal ; but one of the arbitrators was
alleged to have been an interested party, and the
arrangement was repudiated by the Dutch Volks-
raad. Thus the boundaries of our new province
could not be fixed. Quarrels rose daily, and spread

wider and wider. The native tribes became unsettled. Native subjects of the Transvaal appealed to us for protection ; and of course we gave it. The situation became more strained every day, and there would have been war half a dozen times if the Diamond Fields government could have had the support of any military force. Luckily there were no English troops there, and the Cape Colony would not sanction the use of their own police.

Mr. Southey, who was then Governor of the Diamond Fields, was in many ways a most admirable man. He had been the Colonial Secretary at Cape Town, before the days of responsible government. He was intensely English. He believed in England's mission to establish an Anglo-African empire. He had been a good friend to the natives, and the natives everywhere liked and trusted him. He was awkwardly placed at the Diamond Fields, with the two Dutch States on either side of him, and a colony which would not help him behind. A demand for troops from England he knew would be most unwelcome. Mr. Southey was a person of resource ; he looked to his coloured friends, the native chiefs. Hitherto the rule in South Africa had been that fire-arms should not be supplied to the natives. It was a very good rule, as we have lately found to our cost. But natives unarmed would not have been of much service as against the Dutch.

Native labour was wanted at the mines ; the chiefs wanted rifles and powder. The two wants corresponded to one another, and trade and politics could be combined. The chiefs were invited to send their young men to the fields ; the young men, when they returned, might carry back arms and ammunition. They were invited further to declare themselves British subjects, and Mr. Southey calculated that in this way he would be able to hem the Transvaal completely round.

The negotiations went swimmingly on. Diamonds were dug out in enormous quantities. Half a million rifles and ammunition were supplied in four or five years to the chiefs and their subjects. It was thus that Cetewayo and the Zulus got the guns from which we suffered at Isandwana. It was thus that Secocoeni was furnished, whom Sir Garnet Wolseley has just brought to reason—and the Kafirs and the Basutos, and the Korannas, and Griquas, and Bechuanas, with one and all of whom we have since had to fight. Our own loss has been considerable ; they, poor wretches, themselves have been slaughtered in thousands.

This arming of the natives at the Diamond Fields was of course known to the Free State Government, and they could not have been ignorant of the motive of it. They tried to stop it. The road by which the waggons with the arms came to the fields passed through Free State territory. By the law of the Republic no arms might be introduced into the country without permission. The Free State patrols seized the waggons. The English High Commissioner threatened and bullied. The louder the language of the High Commissioner the more obstinate became the Dutch. Ultimatums were sent, with demands for redress, and in terms which seemed deliberately intended to bring on war.

The first spark of actual fire from this arming of the natives broke out in Natal. In the upper part of that Colony, under the Drachenberg Mountains, there resided a refugee Zulu chief named Langalabalele. This potentate, like the rest, had sent young men of his tribe to work at the mine. Having served their time they bought guns, as others did, and carried them home ; having purchased them with the sanction of a British Governor, and with the money which they had themselves earned, they expected to be allowed to keep them. The Natal magistrates ordered that the guns should be brought in and registered ; those that were produced were not returned to the owners, and they naturally refused to bring in any more. The Governor of Natal sent for the chief. The chief was afraid of being killed, and made an excuse to stay at home. The Colony fell into a panic. Governors, judges, magistrates, clergy, people, all assumed that there was to be a rebellion, and they would be murdered in their beds. Instead of sending up half a dozen policemen and arresting the chief, the Colony flew to arms. Native savages who were at feud with Langalabalele were invited to help, with a promise of plunder. The Governor headed the Colonial army in person, and fire and sword was carried through the whole district.

The chief and the most active of his followers fought their way out into Basutoland, where they were afterwards taken. The rest, with the women and children, hid themselves in caves, where the native contingent followed them. In these caves hundreds of poor creatures, women and children among them, were killed. The rest were carried off as prisoners : some to the gaol at Maritzburg ; some dispersed, to work as convicts on the farms. Langalabalele himself was brought back to Natal, where he was tried for treason, and sentenced to imprisonment for life.

The Cape Colony, which had been almost as much excited as its small neighbour, gave its approval to what had been done. The Cape Ministers agreed to take charge of the terrible State prisoner; and he was sent to the penal station at Robbin Island, at the mouth of Table Bay. Here the matter might have rested had it not been for the courage and honourable feeling of one man. To the disgraceful unanimity of Natal sentiment a single exception alone was found. One man remained—

> Unshaken, unreduced, unterrified ;
> Nor number, nor example with him wrought
> To swerve from right or change his constant mind.

It was no light matter to stand alone against an infuriated population, and tell them to their faces that they had been cowards and brutes—yet this Bishop Colenso dared to do. He not only spoke the truth in South Africa ; he was determined that it should be known in England. He collected evidence ; he printed it, and sent it Home ; he followed it himself, amidst the curses of his Colonial fellow-countrymen, to carry his complaint before the Imperial Government.

This was the state of things in the British possessions at the Cape of Good Hope when the late Administration went out of office and Lord Carnarvon became Secretary for the Colonies. I am not going to deliver a panegyric upon Lord Carnarvon. I shall have to complain of him too before I have done ; but I can only say that if the Colonies were consulted in the choice of the Colonial Minister, Lord Carnarvon would remain in Downing Street for the rest of his life.

Naturally enough when he took up his work the state of things in South Africa drew his attention. I happened to mention to him that I was about to travel, and was undecided where to go. He told me that he was perplexed by the reports which reached him from the Cape of Good Hope. Natal had been in conflagration ; trouble was growing about the Diamond Fields ; evidently mischief was at work of some kind. He said he should like to hear from some unprejudiced person what it all meant, and what was the cause of it. He suggested that if I wished to turn my travels to some account I might make a tour through South Africa, of course on my own responsibility, and tell him what I thought about it.

It was in this way that I came to be concerned in these matters, and that I am now speaking to you about them here in Edinburgh. The proposal suited me well enough. Lord Carnarvon gave me letters, and I went out in the summer of 1874, and reached Cape Town in September. I have no leisure just now for the picturesque. Cape Town is a wonderfully beautiful place, and that is all that I can say about it. I found everybody abusing Bishop Colenso. He had just left on his way to England ; we had crossed each other on the voyage. My letters gave me access to the politicians. Mr. Molteno, who was then Premier, was gracious and communicative, and talked to me very freely about the state of the country. He spoke moderately of what had happened in Natal. He thought that there had been far too much violence ; but still there had been a real danger, which could not be neglected. He had felt it his duty to support the Natal Government, as any difference of opinion might excite the natives elsewhere. He protested strongly against English interference ; if the Colony was to bear the burden of its own defence, the Colony must be allowed its own native policy.

This seemed only reasonable.

He next spoke of the Diamond Fields, where I was better informed, for I had been studying the Blue-books, and I could appreciate what Mr. Molteno said. He regretted very strongly the action of the High Commissioner towards the Dutch States. He had himself, he said, opposed the annexation of the Diamond Fields, and if he could he would have prevented it. The quarrel, he thought, was being needlessly and unwisely exasperated. It was not his business to interfere ; but he wished with all his heart that the Imperial Government would adopt more moderate measures, the Dutch people all over the country being greatly irritated. He declined to say what he thought we ought to do. He was cautious of committing himself ; but his condemnation of the proceedings of the High Commissioner was as emphatic as words could make it.

But I was to see the actual scene of the disturbance with my own eyes. I went on to Natal, and thence through the Transvaal, the Diamond Fields, and the Orange Free State. I cannot here describe my journey. I will tell you only the general impressions which I formed. Langalabalele of course was the one subject in Natal. Three of his sons and several hundreds of his tribe were in Maritzburg gaol, as convicts at hard labour. They had not been tried, and they had been in confinement for a year. I saw them and heard their story. The interpreter, who had no prejudice in their favour, was satisfied that they were speaking truth. The account they gave me was the same as that which Bishop Colenso gave, and which England afterwards found to be true.

The Natal people were proud of their achievement, and were furious that it should be called in question. They said that they would have responsible government, like the Cape. A party among them desired to join the Free State and be independent. Responsible government meant that they were to take their own defence upon themselves. That I see is what the English papers now say that they ought to do. Colonists, it is perfectly true, ought to be prepared to defend themselves. But I could wish that the English papers would remember that Natal is not an English colony any more than the Cape. It is only the last, or rather it was then only the last, of the conquests which we had made from the Dutch. There are but ten thousand English there all told. Many of these are no better than the mean whites in the Southern States of the Union. The utmost that they could do would be to bring into the field seven or eight hundred men badly armed and undrilled. We ourselves had to send twenty thousand regular troops there to deal with the Zulus, and the effect of responsible government could only be that they would provoke a war in some foolish panic, and if Natal was still British territory, we should be obliged to go to their help after all, to save the survivors, if any survivors were left. The Dutch would not help them. The Dutch would say that if we chose to take the country we must protect it.

With the finest climate and the finest soil in the world, Natal is a mere wilderness. Here and there a farmer makes a fortune, but generally the whites will not work, because they expect the blacks to work for them. The blacks will not work, because they prefer to be idle; and so no one works at all. Of all the curious enterprises in which British genius has embarked, the acquisition of Natal has been the costliest and the most worthless to us. If we had the courage to allow it to be independent, the Dutch would occupy it again, and save us further trouble. If the colonists remain in the same mind in which I left them, and wish to attach themselves to the Free State, I hope the Imperial Government may see its way towards gratifying their wishes. Then, and only then, shall we have heard the last of Zulu wars.

The Transvaal was much more interesting to me. Of the Transvaal, too, we have heard lately more than we like, and we shall hear further before it is at peace again. The South African Republic, as it was then called, is larger than the United Kingdom. The soil is admirable, the mineral wealth is as varied as it is boundless. There is gold and copper, cobalt, iron, coal, and we know not what besides. Scattered over the surface are eight or nine thousand Dutch households. The Transvaal Boer, when he settles on his land, intends it for the home of his family. His estate is from 6,000 to 20,000 acres, and his wealth is in his sheep and cattle. He comes on the ground in his waggon. He builds sheds or pens for his stock. He encloses three or four acres of garden, carrying a stream of water through it. He plants peaches, apricots, oranges, lemons, figs, apples, pears, olives, and almonds. In a few years they are all in full bearing. The garden being planted, he builds a modest house; a central hall, with a kitchen behind, and a couple of rooms opening out of it at each end. In his hall he places his old chairs and tables, which his father brought from the Colony; his sofa, strung with strips of antelope hide and spread with antelope skins. He has generally but one book—a large clasped Bible, with the births, deaths, and marriages of the family for half a dozen generations on the fly-leaf. He breaks up fifty acres of adjoining land for his corn and green crops. There he lives, and begets a huge family, huge in all senses, for he has often a dozen children, and his boys grow to the size of Patagonians. When a son or daughter marries, another house is built for them on the property ; fresh land is brought under tillage ; and the Transvaal is thus being gradually filled up in patriarchal fashion by a people who know nothing of the world, and care nothing for it ; who never read a newspaper, whose one idea beyond their own concerns is hatred of the English, but who are civil and hospitable to English travellers and sportsmen. They are a proud stubborn race, free, and resolute to remain free, made of the same stuff as their ancestors who drove the Spaniards out of Holland.

I stayed with more than one of them. The beds (I may say this for them) were scrupulously clean, the food plain and abundant. Before and after meals there is a long grace. The day begins with a psalm, sung by the girls. They are strict Calvinists, ignorant, obstinate, and bigoted. But even Calvinism has its merits. They are, I suppose, not unlike what Scotch farmers were two hundred years ago. I enquired much about the slavery which was said to prevail there. I never saw a slave or anything like one. If they were not afraid of us, I daresay they would treat the natives as their countrymen do in Java, but otherwise they are not unkind to them. By far the most thriving native villages which I saw in South Africa were in the neighbourhood of the Dutch towns. The worst and most miserable was at Port Elizabeth—the great English commercial capital —where notwithstanding the coloured people have votes at the elections.

At Pretoria, the seat of their government, I found their Raad or Parliament in session. There was great agitation, for the High Commissioner had just demanded a sum of money as compensation for some trifling injury. The Raad had refused to pay it, and were waiting to see what would happen. There was much anger too at the arming of the native tribes, and the other disputes which had risen out of the Diamond Fields affair. The huts of the chiefs were said to be stacked with rifles, like barrack rooms. The President, Mr. Burgers, was the person whom I had chiefly come to see. He and the High Commissioner had been cannonading each other with fiery despatches, and I wanted to know what he was like.

The chief of the Transvaal Boers was anything but a Boer himself. He was an accomplished, clever, well-educated gentleman. He was gracious and agreeable. He professed to wish to be on good terms with the English; but I doubted if he meant it. He was credited with the ambition of being a South African Washington. He was in treaty with the Portuguese for a railway to Delagoa Bay. He had corresponded with Holland. I believe that he had even approached Prince Bismarck. He talked of a Confederation of the South African States, but when I asked him under what flag it was to be, I got no clear answer. Evidently his opinion was that English rule in those countries was near its end. He I think understood the giving responsible government to the Cape as a prelude to our retiring from it. He supposed us to have concluded that after the opening of the Suez Canal we did not now require the Cape, and were about to abandon it. Had this been so the Washington of South Africa would have had an easy task before him. We had not deserved to find a friend in President Burgers, and we have not found one.

His countrymen did not share the soaring views of the President, and rather laughed at him. They complained bitterly enough of the High Commissioner. They thought that the High Commissioner was deliberately picking a quarrel with them as an excuse for annexation. They were alarmed with good reason at the arming of the native tribes. They had not much hope of peace. But if they could be dealt with fairly, if they were secure of their independence, and if their coloured subjects were not encouraged to rebel against them, they were ready to make reasonable concessions in their mode of managing the natives, and to meet our wishes in other ways.

The irritation was hotter as I approached the Diamond Fields. Farmers clamoured that there was no safety for life or property. As long as the frontier was unsettled, there could be neither magistrates nor police. The chiefs might rise at any moment and burn their houses over their heads. One English settler whom I met at Christiana told me that he was ashamed of his country. I reached at last the famous mine itself. I wish I had time to describe it. The spot itself is a geological miracle. Twenty millions' worth of diamonds have been dug out of it in the last ten years, and no one knows how many more may be left. The town is like a squalid Wimbledon camp. Bohemians of all nations are gathered there like vultures about a carcase. They may be the germ of a great future colony, or the diamonds may give out to-morrow, and they may disappear like a locust swarm. It is impossible to say. The diggers were in a state of incipient insurrection when I arrived : they rebelled openly a few months after, and troops were sent from Cape Town to quiet them. It was the old grievance: with tens of thousands of natives about them, all with guns in their hands, they could not protect their property or sleep quietly in their beds.

My own business was to enquire into the circumstances of the annexation. Half the diggers openly called it robbery, and would have preferred to belong to the Free State. I enquired what had become of Waterboer, the Griqua chief, in whose name we had occupied the place. It appeared that we had cracked the nut, kept the kernel, and given Waterboer the shell. He was away somewhere on a slip of wilderness which had been allowed for himself and his tribe. We had taken away the diamond mine from the Free States on the ground that it belonged to Waterboer; we had then turned out Waterboer and kept it ourselves. Across the lines of the original dispute appeared the figures of persons who had been speculating in land; of some who had made great fortunes; of others who had missed the fortunes, and were ready to split on their luckier rivals. I was in a spider's web spun out of a thousand cross twinings, and where the truth was I could not pretend to judge. I asked one man who was behind the scenes to tell me whether Waterboer's claims had any basis in them. ' Not a fraction,' he said; ' the whole business has been a trick and a swindle. I will prove it so before any arbitrator in the world.'

My own conclusion, after hearing all that could be said, was that I was among a people whose only language on the subject was an infinite conjugation of the verb to lie. As the witnesses flatly contradicted each other, half of them must have lied. I could only regret that the English good name had been soiled by contact with so dirty a business, and we had broken our solemn word too. We have heard much lately about treaties and the faith of treaties. In modern European history no treaty has been ever broken with more deliberate shamelessness than the treaty of Aliwal was broken by us when we annexed the Diamond Fields.

I had still to visit Bloemfontein, the capital of the Orange Free State itself, about seventy miles from the mine. The President, Mr. Brand, I found in no better humour towards England than his brother President at Pretoria. President Burgers was smooth and polished ; you could see no further than the surface of him, and then only the outside objects reflected upon it. President Brand was a blunt straightforward Dutchman, who said what he meant, and was incapable of uttering a single word which he did not mean. To me, when I first saw him, he spoke with dignity and some sternness. The English, a great powerful nation, had been pleased, he said, to break faith with a small weak Republic. They had robbed the Orange Free State, and they had justified themselves by charging the Free State with crimes which it had not committed. He had asked for the arbitration of a foreign Power ; and he had been told that England would not submit her actions to the judgment of foreigners ; he had tried other means of obtaining redress, but they had all failed. He had sent round a protest to the Great Powers, but he could not pretend to resist by force. His people would have resisted, but he had forbidden them ; he would not sanction needless bloodshed. I found that he believed that there was a real Providence in this world, and that an unjust action would not be allowed to prevail.

It was not for me to admit that my own Government had been as unrighteous as President Brand maintained. He, on his part, did not seem to care much whether we came to an arrangement with him or not. He thought, like President Burgers, that our day was nearly over in South Africa. History, he said, showed that all colonies became independent sooner or later. Meanwhile, I suppose he relied on his friends in the Cape Parliament. They could not undo the annexation, but they would protect him from further violence.

Mr. Brand had discharged his resentment upon me as the first Englishman that came in his way; I liked him none the worse for it, and after a few days we became more intimate. He wished to go into his injuries in detail. As well as I could I avoided this. I told him that whether the annexation had been justifiable or not, there would now be an insuperable difficulty in undoing it; but I was sure that the English Government had no bad intentions against him, and that if he could suggest any other way in which good feeling could be restored between us, I believed the Government would meet him half way.

With all their stubbornness the Dutch have a vein of sentiment in them. Mr. Brand seemed to think that his people would be satisfied if we would acknowledge that we had done them wrong. He did not ask to have the mine restored to him, he knew that it was impossible. A fair boundary, with some trifling compensation, would meet his wishes ; and in return he said, like the Boers in the Transvaal, that if we wished it he would then make some modifications in his native administration. He was already, indeed, trying experiments in this direction, and going as far as he dared. Part with his independence, however, he never would. He was sworn to maintain it, and he would maintain it. The friend and ally of England he was willing to be ; its subject never.

That is the true Boer feeling; and no threats, no cajoling, no force, no interest will ever alter it. Such a feeling, I think, deserves to be respected.

I much liked President Brand. He appeared to me a just, upright man, who would stand by his

engagements and never utter untrue words. I
thought, for myself, that the support and friendship
of such a man would contribute more to the peace
and welfare of the English parts of South Africa
than a hundred miserable diamond holes.

The English Church, you may have heard, has a
considerable establishment at Bloemfontein. It is
of advanced Ritualistic type, with which I have no
great sympathy. A leading member of it, however,
who is a man of ability, was good enough to call on
me, and to give me his view of the situation. The
English Government, he said, was making itself
so hated by the Dutch of the Free State, that, unless
there was a change, all the English there might have
to leave it. Either the High Commissioner must
follow up his threats by annexing the province, or
means must be found of making up the quarrel.
Which of these two methods would be more politic
this gentleman did not express an opinion.

My road down from Bloemfontein to the sea took
me through the eastern or English province of the
colony. There I found no sympathy with the so-
called Dutch wrongs. Englishmen like to be masters
wherever they are. They approved of the annexation of the Diamond Fields. They were making
their fortunes by the trade which had sprung up.
The eastern settlers so little liked the Dutch that at
this time they were demanding a division of the

colony into an eastern and western province. They were outvoted in the Cape Parliament by the western Dutch representatives. They felt as Ulster would feel if the Act of Union was repealed and there was an Irish Parliament again. The Ulster Protestants would be always in a minority, and would ask for a separate legislature.

Their testimony, therefore, was the more valuable when they protested universally against the worrying, harassing policy which had been pursued towards the Free States by the High Commissioner. If it did not mean annexation, it was as absurd as it was mischievous. As to the actual differences, they said that there were none which could not be settled in an afternoon, if two or three sensible men from the colony, and as many from Bloemfontein and Pretoria, could be brought together to talk matters over. If we did not intend to suppress the Republics and reclaim them under the British flag, it was high time that something of the kind should be done.

Thus rose the proposal for a Conference, of which I shall tell you more in the next Lecture. I have now only a few more words to add about a Constitutional hurricane which had broken out at Cape Town since I left it, and which I found raging in full fury when I reached it on my way back to England.

Bishop Colenso had gone home. He had laid the circumstances of the Langalabalele outrage before the

Colonial Office; he had produced his evidence—and even without his evidence the official record was itself sufficient to show the monstrous character of the whole proceedings. The country, careless as it is in Colonial matters, had spoken out. The Government did not need to be urged; the good name of our Administration was at stake. The Governor of Natal was recalled, and a despatch was sent to the Cape Ministry requiring that the chief should be removed from the convict station, and be provided for in a more decent manner.

Ministers and people at the Cape were sore and irritated. They thought that they had done a fine thing, and they were told that it was a wrong and foolish thing. They had received responsible government; the Cape was theirs, and it was for them to decide how it ought to be managed. They had not asked for responsible government; it had been forced upon them, to save England expense and trouble. If the natives supposed that when they thought themselves aggrieved they might appeal to the Queen and Ministers at Home, it would be impossible for the Colonial Ministers to maintain their authority. They had replied to Lord Carnarvon with a minute expressing their regret that they could not carry out his wishes. I do not blame them; I blame the system. I believe responsible government to be totally unsuited to the circumstances of South Africa. They had thought so themselves ; but having got it, they naturally insisted upon their rights.

Mr. Molteno, when I called on him, was much disinclined to give way. But he saw that English opinion was excited ; he understood that a collision with the Imperial authorities would be prejudicial to the colony, and that in the end he would be obliged to yield. He was satisfied with his protest, and he empowered me to tell Lord Carnarvon that when the Cape Parliament met he would endeavour to carry out his wishes.

We had little further conversation on the Diamond Fields question. I told him the impressions which I had myself formed ; his own opinion I had already heard from him, and he said not a word to induce me to think that he had altered it.

Here ended my first visit to the Cape, and in closing this Lecture I will sum up the results.

The annexation of the Diamond Fields, whether it was a crime or not, had been a blunder. We had exasperated the whole Dutch population at a moment when the change in the form of government ought to have made us anxious to conciliate them ; we had quarrelled with the two free Republics ; we had broken through our old policy, and entangled ourselves in fresh complications with the natives beyond the Orange River, and we had no longer the revenue of the Cape at our command to help us in dealing with them.

We had broken a treaty; we had damaged our reputation for good faith—and all this without one qualifying advantage. The disorders required instant settlement ; and the alternative lay before us, either violently to annex the Free States and take the responsibility of them on ourselves, or to find some honourable means of arranging our differences with them.

On the prospect of trouble with the natives I could not tell what to think. The excuse for the treatment of Langalabalele was the imminence of insurrection. If the danger was real it had been increased by the needless cruelty, and the distribution of guns among them was incomprehensible folly. Some rational and consistent system of management was evidently desirable. There was one policy in the Cape Colony ; another in Natal ; another in the Free States ; and another at the Diamond Fields. If the Cape Government was right, and there was an actual likelihood of a combined rebellion of Kafirs and Zulus, it was high time that the whole subject should be prudently thought over.

With these conclusions I returned to England.

LECTURE II.

In my first lecture I described to you the state of
South Africa as it was five years ago. You will
have seen that dragons' teeth had been sown broad-
cast. I have now to show how those teeth sprang
up ; how we have had wars on wars, and killed
thousands of innocent people, and annexed more
territories, and spent millions of money, and are
now looking in one another's faces and wondering
how it all came about.

On coming home I reported my impressions to
Lord Carnarvon. He was wise, cautious, and in
many ways slow to agree with me. Like other
Colonial Ministers, he had inherited a prejudice
against the Boers, and he did not give it up because I told him that they were like the Ayrshire
Covenanters. He respected the office of which he
was at the head. He could not accept my opinion
about the annexation of the Diamond Fields, or
believe that his predecessors could have been taken
in by a set of land-sharpers.

The policy of the Colonial Office does not change

E

as Ministers change. If the Colonies were subject to alternations of treatment as Liberals or Conservatives go in and out of power, their connection with us would soon be worn through. In prudence as well as honour, each Secretary of State follows as far as he reasonably can on the lines which he finds laid down ; and Lord Carnarvon had a higher reliance on the judgment of Lord Kimberley than he could possibly have upon mine.

But it was plain that things were going wrong at the Cape. Lord Kimberley had not intended to set up a new Crown Colony across the Orange River, or to quarrel with the Free States on account of it. The Diamond Mine had been meant as a present to the Cape Colony : the Cape Colony declined to touch it. The annexation had irritated the whole Dutch population. Our precious acquisition was causing indefinite trouble and danger ; while to ourselves it was totally useless.

Lord Carnarvon attached great importance to what I told him of the opinion of Mr. Molteno ; and although it was now impossible to restore the mine to its old owners, it was clear that means ought to be found for reconciling the Dutch to our keeping it.

The Colonial Office had long been anxious to confederate the States of South Africa, and to form a self-governed Dominion there like that which had succeeded so well in Canada. If the Republics could be induced to join, all difficulty would be at an end. The mine would still be English, to whatever province it might be attached. The advantages of such an arrangement were obvious at home, and we are apt to assume that, our views being always reasonable, other people will see things as we do. Other people, unfortunately, are not always reasonable. The Dutch States I knew to be most unreasonably fond of independence. The Cape Dutch everywhere object to our presence at the Cape in any shape. The two Republics were free of us, and I thought it most unlikely that with their own consent they would come back under our flag. They were ready, if they were well treated, for an alliance with us; they were willing to modify their native administration to please us. The Queen's subjects they would not agree to be for any bribe that we might hold out to them.

Nor did I think the colony would like Confederation. At present it had all the advantages of the situation. The trade of the interior States passed through the colonial ports; duties were levied there on every bale of goods that passed up to the Free States and the Diamond Fields. The colony kept those duties; it keeps them still. Under confederation it would have to account for them. The colony was rich; it was out of harm's way; Natal might be in danger from the natives; the Cape Colony was in little danger, if in any. Why should the Cape make itself responsible for keeping the peace in Natal and in the interior States? The colony, I thought, would relieve us of the Diamond Fields if the dispute with the Free States could be first arranged—more than this I did not think it would do.

Perhaps my views of what was probable were coloured by my conviction of what was right. I did not then, and I do not now, think that we ought to establish a self-governed Dominion in South Africa. Self-government in South Africa means the government of the natives by the European colonists: and that is not self-government. The parallel with New Zealand does not hold. The Maoris are few and are dying out; the Kafirs and Zulus are in millions and are increasing faster than the whites. The Europeans, I do not doubt, could control them: but they could and would control them only by measures which Great Britain would never allow to be carried out in the Queen's name. It is agreed that we must keep a garrison still at Cape Town to protect the naval station, and as long as there is a British regiment in South Africa it will be employed, if we insist on setting up a Dominion-Parliament there, in supporting a system of government which for half a century we have repudiated and condemned.

If a line could be drawn across from Table Bay to False Bay, if the Cape Town peninsula was ours and ours only, and the whole of the rest of the country was entirely independent of us, as I heartily wish it was, then I would leave South Africa to the South Africans, white or coloured, to shape out its own fortunes; the responsibility would then be theirs. But as long as the government is carried on in the Queen's name the responsibility will cling to us ; and therefore, for myself, I would wait to establish a South African Dominion till the law should know no distinction of colour, and the black races can be enfranchised, as the slaves have been enfranchised in the Southern States of the American Union.

Whether, however, Confederation was or was not eventually practicable, it could not be thought of till a disposition had been shown to satisfy the complaints of the Dutch. It was not easy for Lord Carnarvon to tell Parliament that we had been doing wrong and must make amends for it; nor was he himself satisfied that we had done wrong. To him the question was one of prudence. Would it not be prudent and politic, things being as they were, to make some concession to Dutch feeling? A Parliamentary debate on the subject was not desirable. The sins of the Boers, real or imaginary, would be brought up in the course of it. It was the belief then among members of Parliament—it is the belief now of nine-tenths of them—that the Boers exist only to the north of the Orange River. They will not understand that two-thirds of the inhabitants of the Cape Colony are Boers, and that every light word which they utter is dwelt upon with resentment in every Dutch household. The object was to find some general ground of action which the country would accept as satisfactory without irritating discussions about broken treaties or our having taken possession of other people's property.

As I said in the last lecture, a Conference of Delegates had been suggested at the Cape itself as the best way out of the difficulty. It seemed certain that with Mr. Molteno's assistance some plan might be struck out which would give satisfaction in South Africa, and if presented in the name of the Colony would be satisfactory here at home. No party in England could wish to persevere in a course of action from which we had nothing to gain, and which South Africa generally condemned. If a conference in which Dutch and English colonists were equally represented recommended that some compensation should be made to the Orange Free State, compensation could easily be made.

Lord Carnarvon resolved to make the experiment, and he addressed a despatch to the Governor of the Cape proposing a Conference. To have said much about the Diamond Fields would have implied a confession that some wrong had been done. Of this Lord Carnarvon himself was imperfectly convinced, and therefore it was alluded to only in a single paragraph as requiring consideration. The main body of the despatch referred to the management of the natives. Lord Carnarvon, supposing naturally that there must be some foundation for the fears which had been made the excuse of the violence in Natal, invited the representatives of the different Colonies and States to give him their opinion on the whole system of native administration, in order to prevent the recurrence of fresh outrages. A paragraph, most modest, indeed, but still with a clear meaning, was introduced at the end, intimating that if the Colonies and States saw their way to a Confederation it would be heartily approved at home.

Advice was all that was asked for, and advice only about action to be taken beyond the colonial frontiers. No one dreamt of interfering with the native policy of the Cape Colony. Who could have supposed that an invitation so mild, so considerate, would have been taken as an insult by the Colonial Ministry and have thrown all South Africa into convulsions?

South Africa must have been in a highly sensitive condition.

Mr. Molteno had honourably carried out his engagements to provide better treatment for Langalabalele. He had introduced a Bill for his removal from the convict island. There had been a tempest about it in the Cape Parliament, and the Bill had been carried with great difficulty. Lord Carnarvon had been charged with interfering with the liberties of the Colony. An eloquent patriot had said to me that an English Secretary of State has as much right to desire anything to be done in the Cape Colony as in " yonder star," pointing to a planet that was shining down upon us. In requesting Mr. Molteno to give his assistance on the Conference, Lord Carnarvon had innocently named also the senior member for Port Elizabeth, Mr. Paterson. As the object was to obtain impartial advice on the dispute with the Dutch States, he naturally thought the presence desirable of an influential representative from the English side of the Colony. This gave mortal offence. Mr. Molteno was affronted because he, the Premier, was placed on a level with a gentleman who happened to be the leader of the Opposition. It was conceived that Lord Carnarvon was insidiously meditating a division of the provinces. In certain states of mind, the more absurd the notion that enters into it, the more credible it is.

I had given Mr. Molteno credit for more understanding than it seems he possessed. As I was myself to take part in the Conference as Lord Carnarvon's representative, I wrote to Mr. Molteno privately at the time that the despatch went out, explaining the objects of it and expressing the confidence with which

Lord Carnarvon relied on his assistance. Special care had been taken to meet Mr. Molteno's particular views. Indeed, Mr. Molteno's own expressions had been the occasion of the proposal. I suppose on the other side of the globe where the sun at midday is in the north, and grapes and strawberries ripen at Christmas, the processes of reason are subject to similar obliquities. I went out myself a fortnight after the despatch had gone. On my arrival I learnt the reception which it had met with. Mind, the only object of it had been to ask the advice of the leading Cape statesmen how to arrange the quarrel between the English Government and the Dutch States in the manner which would give most satisfaction in the Colony. This first—and then to adjust the native administration beyond the Cape Border as to prevent any fresh collision between the Cape Ministry and the Imperial Government.

The despatch had arrived while the Cape Parliament was sitting. There was no haste, for it was to sit five weeks longer. I was myself to follow in a few days. If there was any doubt as to Lord Carnarvon's object, I should be on the spot to explain. The Ministers did not wait. They laid the despatch on the table with a minute condemning the interference of the Imperial Government with the affairs of the Colony. The despatch itself was read amidst shouts of laughter. Violent resolutions were passed declaring that it was for the Colony to decide when it was expedient to raise questions affecting the interests of South Africa. Lord Carnarvon's action was interpreted as a sinister attempt to involve the Colony in the quarrel with the Free State. The Dutch were of course more furious than ever. The Conference was peremptorily rejected, one prominent orator describing the vote which they gave, as a slap in the face to Lord Carnarvon : another asking who Lord Carnarvon was ; he might be a minister in England : he was no minister in the Cape Colony.

I cannot explain all this. A few gentlemen—my friend Mr. Paterson among them—remonstrated, but to no purpose. I arrived to find the whole matter apparently finished. For myself, I was told that I was in a constitutional country, and that my mouth was closed—a very odd inference. The Cape Town people, with a sense of fair play, invited me to a dinner to give explanations: I was officially informed that I had no right to give them.

I am sorry to talk so much about so insignificant a person as myself. But I cannot help it. I am simply telling a curious story which had important consequences. I was perplexed, but I thought that there must be some mistake. I supposed that Mr. Molteno could not have read my letter to him. But he received me when I called upon him—I cannot say discourteously (Mr. Molteno cannot be discourteous), but in a way which showed me that at least I had not understood the temper of Colonial politicians. Lord Carnarvon, he said, had raised a storm in the Colony which would last for years. He had been himself treated with disrespect. The time had not come for Confederation, and he would not have it argued. If the Imperial Government had got into a scrape with the Dutch, they must get out of it as they could. I reminded him of his own words. He had himself said that he wished that the Imperial Government would adopt a more conciliatory policy towards the Dutch. Lord Carnarvon only desired the Colony and Mr. Molteno himself to tell him how they would like him to act. To my extreme surprise, he replied: ' Oh, we don't care. Go on as you are doing. It is nothing to us what you do.'

A light broke upon me. Mr. Molteno wished for Confederation, but a Confederation on his own terms. He wished us to have the odium and trouble of forcing the Free States back under the British flag, while he himself affected to regret it. When the work was done, he would then offer to take them in under the Constitution. A Dominion formed in this way would simply be a Dutch State reconstituted, filled with a determined and just resentment against the English Government. South Africa on such terms would not be worth our possessing. If this was Mr. Molteno's purpose, it was neither fair nor tolerable. I hinted my suspicions to him. He did not admit that I was right, but he did not deny it. He simply said that he had made up his mind to have nothing to do with the Conference, and that the question could not be reopened. I asked him if he would lay what I had said before the Parliament. He said that there was no occasion for it. I enquired whether I was at liberty to speak at the dinner. He answered that it would be at my own risk. It would be unconstitutional, and the Governor would not support me.

Meanwhile the worst effect had been produced outside. The simple Dutch people had accepted the debates in Parliament as a detection of Lord Carnarvon's wicked intentions towards them. Several Dutch gentlemen of consequence represented to me that if Lord Carnarvon's object had really been what I declared it to be, it was of the utmost importance that I should make it known.

I had to consider what I would do. The word unconstitutional had a terrible sound. I might have addressed a letter to the Governor, and desired him to lay it before Parliament. But the Governor could only act constitutionally by the advice of his Ministers. Mr. Molteno had distinctly told me that the matter should not be brought before Parliament again, so that road was closed—besides, a letter could be misinterpreted as easily as a despatch. Moreover, free speech is a right of the British subject. I had come out to take part in a Conference, and so far might be considered an official person ; but the Conference had been rejected, and the disability could not cling to me for ever. The only real remedy for the situation was to go myself among the Dutch, to tell them what Lord Carnarvon's purpose was, and answer any questions which they might ask me. If I was doing wrong, the responsibility would only be my own ; while I saw that very great mischief would follow if I went home without speaking. The poor Dutch are very easily persuaded that an English Minister has had bad intentions towards them, and no disclaimers following after an interval of months would remove the effect. Mr. Molteno accused me of lending myself to the Parliamentary Opposition. On the contrary, I acted at the entreaty of the leaders of the Dutch party, who up to that moment had been Mr. Molteno's strongest supporters.

I spoke at Cape Town. I travelled through the Dutch province. I told the people as simply as possible why I had come out; and the effect was singular. Those phlegmatic Hollanders are the most impressionable people in the world when they hear a word of kindness. Lord Carnarvon's despatch as I explained it was the first gracious message which they had heard from an English Minister since we took

their country from them. They followed me about
in their carts; they dressed up their towns; they
came to meet me at cross roads. They forced me to
tell my story over again, as if they could not hear
it too often. Everything was forgotten. Their
brothers in the Free States had been thought of
kindly, and were to be treated with justice. Even
Confederation seemed now no longer impossible. The
British flag would cease to be a grievance, if there
was fair dealing. They would be one people again.
This was all very curious. I only wanted the Conference. I doubted if the present humour would
last, but it was not my business to check it. I, too,
thought at that time that a Confederation brought
about by conciliation might perhaps be a happy thing
for the country. At any rate it was something to be
looked forward to in the future, and conciliation
towards the Dutch and the natives was the safest road
to it.

Afterwards I went to Port Elizabeth and Grahams-
town. There also the people had their enthusiasms
—but for a different object. They, too, wanted Confederation, but it was that they might be relieved
from Western domination and have an administration
of their own. They catechised me privately on this
point. At the risk of losing their help, I told them
that Lord Carnarvon had never thought of separat-
ing the provinces. Confederation rather than separa-

tion was the object of the Imperial Government.
Still, any claims that they might have would of course
be considered when the terms of it were arranged.
The Conference and the settlement of the Dutch
question was the point first to be aimed at. Whenever I spoke of Confederation, it was as of something
remote, which they must bring about for themselves.

The excitement spread over the whole country.
Almost every town passed resolutions condemning
the ungracious reception of Lord Carnarvon's proposal. The Ministers were very angry. They recalled the Parliament—which was exactly what I
wished them to do. Their papers continued to
accuse me of all kinds of crimes. I did not care
much about that ; I was certain that if Parliament
met another tone would have to be assumed. For
myself I felt that I had done all that was necessary.
I regretted the violence of the agitation. I did not
myself wish to see a change of Ministry, still less to
be a cause of it ; for I still thought Mr. Molteno to
be the best Premier that the Colony could provide.
I had therefore written to Lord Carnarvon that I did
not know whether I had done right or wrong ; but
that as the Colony had so fully expressed its feelings,
his immediate purpose was answered. The discussions in the Colonial press had given him as complete
information as he could have received from a Con-

ference of Delegates, and I did not see that I could myself be of further service.

Well, the Cape Parliament met. I was denounced, as I expected, for being an agitator. The Ministers proposed a resolution condemning, not me only, but Lord Carnarvon also. It was the old Parliament, the members of which had already committed themselves. They wished to support Mr. Molteno as far as they dared ; but he found that he could not carry this resolution, and he withdrew it. He produced another in a milder form. On this it appeared that the numbers would be equal. There would then have been a change of Ministry, a dissolution, and an appeal to the country. It might have been better had it come to this. I cannot say. Certainly I did not wish it at the time. I had desired to smooth matters, not to irritate them. I proposed to Mr. Molteno, through a common friend, to confine the questions to be discussed at the Conference to the Diamond Fields affair only. He might name his own delegates ; or, if he pleased, I would be content with the opinion of the Judges of the Colony. He would not agree, and extremities seemed inevitable ; when there arrived at the critical moment a despatch from England, in which Lord Carnarvon withdrew his proposal for a Conference at the Cape, and invited delegates to meet him in London. Mr. Molteno would still have pressed his resolution ;

but he was informed privately that he must allow a promise to be attached to it, on the part of the Colony, to assist the Imperial Government in settling the differences with the Dutch. Finding that if he refused he would be defeated, he reluctantly consented. He carried his censure on my unfortunate self. But I had gained my object. If the Colony took part in the settlement, the Dutch would either be satisfied or they would no longer be able to throw the blame on the British Government.

With this my own small connection with the affairs of South Africa ended ; and I considered myself happily out of the wood.

For a time things went on well on the new lines. The London Conference came to little or nothing ; but the President of the Orange Free State came to England. The annexation was talked over. Mr. Brand did not insist on an uncomfortable acknowledgment that it had been unjust ; but it was admitted that he had something to complain of : £90,000 was paid to him as compensation, with a promise of £15,000 more if he made a railway from the Orange River to Bloemfontein. Mr. Brand was satisfied ; the Free State was satisfied. The Cape Parliament loyally carried out its engagements, and agreed, now that the dispute was arranged with one at least of the two Republics, to take the Diamond Fields into the Colony. The Imperial Government was relieved of the territory which had slipped so inconveniently into its hands. An actual step was gained in the direction of the so much desired Confederation. As soon as the incorporation was completed, the differences which remained with the Transvaal would be no longer an affair of ours, and would be left to the Colonial authorities.

And yet—how it has all happened I do not know —the Act has remained a dead letter. Through no fault of the Colony, the Diamond Fields still belong to the Crown. We were relieved of our responsibility, but we have chosen to keep it ; not only have we done this, but we have seized the Transvaal itself. The seizure of the Transvaal dragged us into war with the Zulus, with Secocoeni, with Bechuanas, Korannas, Griquas—naked barbarians, but barbarians with guns with which we had ourselves provided them. Sir Bartle Frere, who went out on a mission of peace, rushed at once into war with the Kafirs. The whole interior of South Africa during the last two years has been a scene of blood and frenzy. Thousands of natives have been killed, entire villages have been destroyed. The Dutch, who had half forgotten their wrongs, now hate the name of England worse than they ever hated it. A feeling has risen between the white and black races which makes the jury trials on the frontier a mockery. All Kafir land has been converted into British territory ; but we know not who is to govern it. No revenue can be raised in the Transvaal. Natal and the Diamond Fields are loaded with debt ; we ourselves are waiting humbly to learn from the Chancellor of the Exchequer how much we are to pay for the honour of having murdered twelve thousand of the defenders of Zululand.

Four years ago all South African difficulties were on the point of disappearing—and yet this is our present state. How has it come about ? ' Some one has blundered,' as Mr. Tennyson says of the Balaklava Charge. ' Some one '—I fear a good many *some ones*. But all blunders have their causes. I will explain, as far as I know them, the causes here.

When the Free State dispute was settled, there remained our differences with the Transvaal. We might have handed over the Diamond Fields and these differences together to the Cape Colony. We neglected to do one, and therefore did not do the other.

I spoke in my last lecture of Mr. Burgers, the President of the Transvaal. He had no love for England. I cannot complain of him on that account : we had been arming the native tribes against him and his people, a thing that was neither just nor wise on our part. Angry men are sometimes imprudent. President Brand came for redress to the British Government, and got it. President Burgers was to be the Washington of South Africa ; he looked for friends elsewhere. Gold had been found in the Transvaal. There was a chance at the moment that the Transvaal might prove another California. The President struck a coin with metal from his own diggings, and with his own face upon it. He came to Europe with a box of specimens. He went to Holland. He went to Portugal. He negotiated a loan abroad for a railway to Delagoa Bay. He hoped to tempt Dutch and German emigrants to settle in the Transvaal, to establish relations with the European Powers and to put himself under their protection. We have no avowed Monroe doctrine in South Africa, but we have views on this subject which come to the same thing ; and the President's proceedings were watched with no particular good will. Had he applied to the Secretary for the Colonies like Mr. Brand, his grievances would have been set right, as those of the Free State had been. But his ambition aspired to higher objects. On his return from Europe he made some singular speeches in the Cape Colony. He advised his own people to have as little to do with the English as possible. He set about his railway scheme on one side ; on another he began to use high language to the native chiefs on his borders. He had a dispute with Cetewayo about his boundary. He claimed Secococni as a subject : whether he was right or wrong I do not know. As long as the Transvaal was independent, we took the side of the natives against the President ; as soon as the Transvaal was ours, we changed our views, we went to war with Cetewayo, and we have been fighting with Secococni. The alteration can no doubt be explained in a way that will be satisfactory to ourselves. Outside spectators are perplexed—owing of course to ignorance and prejudice.

Well, the President undertook to reduce Secococni and made a bad hand of it. Ultimately, with the help of some Diamond Field volunteers, he gained some trifling advantages, and Secococni agreed to a peace ; but by this time the storm was thickening all round the Transvaal : Cetewayo and the Zulus threatened it on one side, the Matabeles on another. Secococni was not likely to remain quiet long. The treasury at Pretoria was empty. The Boers had become dissatisfied with the President and would pay no taxes. The railway loan was spent, the State was bankrupt, and there was every prospect of a bloody and desperate struggle between the Dutch and their native neighbours.

Meanwhile the Government at home was anxious to realise the feeling which had arisen in favour of Con-federation. An enabling Bill was passed through Par-liament, in spite of the efforts of the Irish members, and Sir Bartle Frere went out as Governor to carry it into act. The Cabinet was in too great a hurry. Confederations may grow, but they cannot be manufactured. All the Acts of Parliament in the world will not ripen the harvest a day before its time. The Cabinet believed, unluckily, that the harvest was ripe already, and that they had only to gather it. The state of the Transvaal was partly our own fault, for it was we who had supplied the natives with guns and powder. The situation was tempting ; for the Transvaal seemed the key of the political position. With the Transvaal in our hands there could be no more negotiations with other nations. The Orange Free State would be surrounded by British territory, and would soon be tired of its independence. Why not take the Transvaal then ? Nothing would better please the old enemies of the Boers. English settlers and traders there wished it for the security of their property. No one knows less, I think, of the feelings of the Dutch than their English neighbours, and all English people habitually believe what they wish. It seemed a mere act of humanity to step in and prevent a war between the Boers and the natives. Lord Carnarvon, with the entire conviction that the Boers themselves desired it, allowed the Transvaal to be taken over, as it was called, in the Queen's name.

Those who really understood South Africa knew what must follow. If we had wished to gain the affection of the Dutch people for ever, Providence had given us the opportunity. A small loan of money and a public offer of help to the Dutch Republic, if it was in extremities, would have shot the South African States into one as easily as if they had been so many balls of quicksilver. If Lord Carnarvon had wished to do this, English prejudice would perhaps have forbidden him ; but I think he might have waited. If the danger to the Transvaal was as real and as near as Lord Carnarvon was led to believe, the Boers in a few months would have appealed to him for assistance, and he could have made his own terms. They could not then have said that they were annexed against their will. They could not then have said, as they say now, that they did not want our help, and that they could have successfully defended themselves.

Annexation unasked for would certainly revive the bitter feelings of the Dutch in the Cape Colony. It would forfeit all that had been gained by the settlement of the Diamond Fields affair, and it would again entangle the Imperial Government in the con· cerns of the interior of the continent. The Cape Colony would only undertake the defence of the interior frontier, if it was obliged to undertake it. If we chose to take it upon ourselves, they would be only too happy to see us charged with the burden, and Confederation would only be further off than ever. We had just extricated ourselves out of this position by the engagement of the Cape to take the Diamond Fields. Why should we plunge into it again? If the object was to prevent a struggle with the natives, the chances were that the struggle would come not-withstanding. The difference would only be that the business of killing the natives would fall on us and not on the Dutch.

Notwithstanding these objections, the annexation was persisted in, and the Zulu War immediately followed.

It was not the first war which Sir Bartle Frere had begun in South Africa. Sir Bartle Frere had gone out, as I said, to confederate the South African States. If the Cape Colony was to undertake the defence of the country, the object should have been to diminish as far as possible the responsibilities which would be thrown upon the Colony. The Government at home had just added to these responsibilities on one side by taking the Transvaal. Sir Bartle Frere, in his capacity of High Commissioner, made war on Kreli, the chief of the Kafirs, and annexed Kaffraria, add-ing about half a million to the number of natives whom the Colony would be expected to govern. Kaffraria is naturally rich. It is, or it might be, the garden of South Africa. No doubt many of the colonists looked on it with covetous eyes. It is easy to make a war if you wish for it. Kreli had done us no harm. Some difference had risen between Kreli's people and a tribe who were under our protection. It was a mere police case, but perhaps the High Com-

missioner thought that the way to Confederation
would be made more easy if the independent native
chiefs in the neighbourhood of the Colony were
brought into subjection. Demands were made on
Kreli which he could not accept. War followed.
It cost the Colony a million. How much it cost us
I do not know. It spread along the frontier up to
the Kei, and down the Orange River. Vast numbers
of men have been destroyed. Women and children
have been killed in cold blood. Kreli is still at
large, but his country has been taken from him. This
war is but just over. The last stage of it was the
storming of the stronghold of a Basuto chief named
Morosi. Morosi himself was killed.

When the Kafir war was half finished, Sir Bartle
Frere went on to Natal to settle with the Zulus.
The Zulus are the noblest and bravest of all the
African tribes so far as we yet know them. They
and their king Cetewayo had always been good
neighbours to the English in Natal, and as long
as the Boers had the Transvaal it was our policy to
be on good terms with Cetewayo. The Zulus are a
warlike people, as we know to our cost. They were
proud of their independence, and determined to
maintain it, and they kept up a large army. I do
not see that they were to be blamed for this. I
mentioned that there was a disputed frontier between
them and the Boers. The cause of our taking the

Transvaal was to prevent the Boers and the Zulus from fighting. When the Transvaal became ours the frontier had still to be settled. A Commission was appointed to arrange it, one member of which was my distinguished and gallant friend Colonel Durnford, who was killed at Isandwana. The Commissioners reported in favour of the line claimed by the Zulus. But some Dutch farmers had located themselves on the Zulu side of it, and Sir Bartle decided that Cetewayo must be content with his sovereignty, and must leave these Boers in possession of the land. As the Boers were in a bad humour with us for having taken away their liberty, it was thought, perhaps, that a sop of this kind would please them. Cetewayo would not agree to this; and as there was no longer any Transvaal Republic against which his army might be useful, we discovered that he had no need of an army. It had been always an anxiety to the people in Natal; they did not like exerting themselves, or taxing themselves, to keep up a force of their own. I think the force of police which was kept up by Natal amounted to about 200 men. Cetewayo had 40,000 or 50,000. It would be more agreeable to the Natalians, and perhaps Sir Bartle thought that the Cape Colony would be more ready to take charge of Natal, if this army of Cetewayo's was broken up. So Cetewayo was treated as Kreli had been. There was no difficulty in finding an excuse. The Tugela River only divides Natal from Zululand; fugitives from either side were in the habit of crossing to the other. Some Zulu runaways had come over into Natal, and had been pursued and taken back. Reparation might have been demanded fairly; but Cetewayo was told at the same time that, as British territory now lapped him round, his army was unnecessary. If used at all, it could only be used against us. This was very likely true. Cetewayo, seeing us swallowing so much territory, thought it as well, naturally enough, to be on his guard against us; but a reason like this Sir Bartle could not recognise. The Kafir war had brought a larger number of British troops into South Africa than are usually maintained there. The opportunity was a favourable one; and Sir Bartle sent an ultimatum to Cetewayo requiring, among other demands, that his regiments should be disbanded. Of course he knew that the brave, proud chief could give him but one answer. He would have redressed any wrong which had been committed by his people; he could not lay down his arms at the command of a British Governor. A friend of mine lately visited Cetewayo in his prison at Cape Town, and asked him if he did not regret having disobeyed Sir Bartle's commands. Cetewayo replied that had he known all that would happen he would have given the same reply. A brave man might know that he would be beaten, but he would still fight, rather than submit like a coward. His people all felt as he did.

I think you in Scotland ought to have some sympathy with Cetewayo and his Zulus.

I need not go over the story. The war was no child's play. To conquer these naked savages we employed a force almost as large as we sent to Sebastopol. The Zulus did not skulk among caves and forests; they met our breechloaders in the open field with assegais. They were beaten finally at Ulundi ; a thousand of them were reported as killed there : we hear of no wounded—I know not why. It has been said that the wounded were either left to die, or were killed after the battle by our native contingent. Some questions will perhaps be asked hereafter on this subject. I trust, for the honour of the British army, that so horrible a suspicion will be removed.

Meanwhile, the war is over. The colonists have finished off Morosi; Sir Garnet Wolseley has disposed of Secocoeni. There is nominal peace. The Boers in the Transvaal are still sullen. I do not suppose that they will resist the English Government by force so long as British troops are in the province; but they will pay no taxes, and, if I know their character rightly, they will remain in determined, stubborn, silent opposition.

What, then, have we gained by what we have done and spent in the last four years? We have gained a province, which is totally useless to us, against the will of its owners; we have annexed another million of native subjects, when we had more before than we knew what to do with ; we have taught the Kafirs and Zulus that the South Africans are no match for them without the red men from beyond the sea. Let the red men go, and they will have small fear of the South Africans. Now what is to be done? The Prime Minister says that we have taught South Africa a lesson of self-defence. Henceforward she must take care of herself. The First Lord of the Admiralty says that if emigrants choose to push their fortunes in another country, they must be prepared to take the consequences. The newspapers say that as soon as Parliament meets, the Government must be prepared with decisive measures and force South Africa to understand that she must fight her own battles henceforward. Will our kind instructors remember that South Africa, as I said before, is not an English colony? It is a conquered country. We took it from the Dutch for our own purposes. If we tell the Dutch that they must now defend it, they will say, 'Give us back our country', and we are ready to defend it. If you choose to keep it, you must defend it yourselves. You cannot expect us to govern it on your principles and in the name of your Queen.'

We say that South Africa must bear her own

wars. How will this be in detail? The chief danger is in Natal : let the English garrison go, and Natal lies at the Zulus' mercy. Her neighbours, the Dutch, will not lift a finger, nor her own Dutch residents ; the work would fall on the 10,000 English. If they are wise, they will every one of them follow the soldiers into some safer country. They did not make this Zulu quarrel. The Zulus were good neighbours till we made war upon them ; if they are our enemies now, it is our fault, not the colonists' fault. As long as the Government of Natal is carried on in the Queen's name, we must defend it ; and all the vapouring in the world will not relieve us.

In the Transvaal the English authority will last while there is a British regiment there—when the last regiment is withdrawn, the Boers will simply take down the British flag.

Do we rely on the Cape Colony? The Cape Colony will say: 'We will defend ourselves within our own limits as we have hitherto done. We will take charge of the Diamond Fields. We might have done more in time and with proper precautions, if you had left the Transvaal and the Kafirs and Zulus alone. You have multiplied the difficulties of defending South Africa tenfold. You tell us you will not fight our wars henceforward. Your Kafir and Zulu wars were not our wars. You say you thought they would be useful to us : you may have thought so—we did not think so. A few fools may have encouraged you : we, the responsible persons in the Colony, did not encourage you. Our native problem was hard enough for us before ; it is beyond our strength now, and you have no right to thrust it off upon us.'

Are we to force South Africa to unite under the Dominion Act ? I do not see how we can do it, except by threatening to withdraw the troops out of the country altogether. And this we cannot do. We must keep a garrison at Cape Town; and let us say what we please, these troops will not be permitted to stand inactive if natives are murdering colonists, or if colonists are murdering natives. But grant that we can force South Africa into the same position as New Zealand, I say that we have no longer any right to do it. Thanks to our late exploits, half a million Europeans in that country would have under their control nearly six times their number of natives. I do not say that the Europeans could not keep this mass of barbarians in order, but they could do it only by disarming them, by taking their lands from them, by reducing them into the state of complete subjection and dependence into which the Dutch reduce their subjects in Java. It might not come next year or the year after: it would come before many years. And is British opinion prepared to allow it? I am perfectly certain that it is not. We should hold off till we had forgotten the vexation of our present trouble. A generation hence something would happen which would stir public feeling, as Governor Eyre's proceedings in Jamaica did—we should interfere again, and throw everything once more into confusion.

It would be Ireland over again. We annexed Ireland; we sent colonists there to govern it; we gave the colonists a Parliament; we gave them the management of native affairs there. The result was a series of laws which we would not allow to be executed; we had the weakness of an oligarchical administration without its strength, wars, rebellions, confiscations, quarrels with the colonists, quarrels with the native race; misgovernment, poverty, misery; and finally the Ireland that we know, which is the disgrace of British administration. The state of Ireland is no extraordinary mystery. It is as much the product of causes clearly ascertainable as a famine or the cholera. And yet step by step we are treading on the old course, and are creating exactly and literally a second Ireland in South Africa. What would you do, then? I shall be impatiently asked. You will not have our remedy. Suggest something yourself. I should say, first, perhaps that I was glad that I was not Secretary of State, for if I was I should try a hazardous experiment. I should try what justice would do. I would give back the Transvaal to the

Dutch. I would restore Cetewayo to Zululand and Kreli to Kaffraria. I would make them each an apology and give them compensation, and I would in this way do public penance for my own iniquities. I seriously believe that an honest course of this kind would prove in the long run the wisest that we could take.

But as this will not be, we must look to the alternatives. For us the happiest issue by far would be the separation of Table Mountain from the rest of South Africa. We might keep our naval station in our own hands. The remainder might all be independent and might do as it pleased. Or we might suspend the Cape Constitution and place all the States and Colonies under an impartial administration like that of India. Able men with full powers of government could then keep order and do justice there at no cost to this country.

But these expedients also cannot be resorted to. We are the most reasonable people in the world, but nevertheless we are surrounded by enchantments. This or that road may seem open to us and good to travel upon, but a mysterious sign-post warns us that there is no passage that way.

Well then, since when a free constitution has been once granted it cannot be taken back, and since where the British flag has once flown our honour requires that it shall continue to fly, the next best

G

course, 1 think, would be to consider how South
Africa would dispose of itself if it really was made
independent. True political wisdom lies in dis-
cerning the lines in which things are inclined to run
of themselves, and in availing ourselves of the forces
thus generated.

Would South Africa become united if we were
out of the way? I think it would not. There
would be a natural line of cleavage between the
Dutch and English populations. The Eastern Province would separate from the Western, and Natal
and the Eastern Province would draw together.

When the Cape Constitution was granted the
Eastern Province petitioned for separation. The
question was suspended for further consideration,
and therefore, if the Eastern Province remains now
in the same mind, the petition could be constitutionally acted upon. The Western Dutch Province
could then be left entirely undisturbed to manage
its own affairs. No native problem could rise
there to call for British interference, and in a short
time the Orange Free State would naturally unite
with it. The Eastern Province and Natal would
have Kaffraria between them, and Zululand as the
eastern frontier. On them would fall the whole
pressure of the native administration. For a province so placed a new Constitution could be formed,
in which we should ourselves, at least for a time,

bear a part. In return for assistance we should have a legitimate voice in the management, and if we did not entirely escape the burden of this beautiful South African property of ours, we could at least be relieved of part of it.

This plan seems to me to be a feasible one if the English party in the Colony themselves consent to it; and it might be accompanied with guarantees and securities for the good treatment of the natives, which would be simply impossible under a Dominion two-thirds of which would be Dutch. But the wind changes quickly in those countries. It blows east to-day and west to-morrow. The colony which five years ago was like an ill-matched man and wife may now be linked together in the bonds of tender affection.

In that case ' we have made our bed,' as they say, ' and we must lie upon it.' We have chosen for our own amusement to take Kaffraria, to take the Transvaal, to conquer Zululand. It will be bad for us in every way to be led to suppose that we can send troops and annex territories wholesale, and then thrust the trouble of them upon others. If we eat an unwholesome supper we must not expect our neighbours to suffer the indigestion. We must bear the indigestion ourselves, and it is very good that we should. We shall be more careful what we eat hereafter. I have been considering nothing but our own interests. But the natives, too, have a right to be considered. If we invade them and overthrow their chiefs, the least that we can do is to provide them with a tolerable' government in return. A tolerable government means one that shall be just and strong. The Colony cannot provide such a government. We can—and we only. The natives will resist the colonists, because they believe that they are a match for them. British magistrates they will not resist, because they know that the power of Great Britain lies behind. I am sorry that circumstances or our own folly have forced us into an expensive position. But being there we must honourably make the best of it. Kaffraria, Basuto Land, Natal, and the Protectorate over Zululand will then remain in the hands of the Crown, and the Crown will have to keep them till the natives can be sufficiently educated to be trusted with the franchise. The experiment can thus be tried whether any of the native races in South Africa are capable of real civilisation. Under a South African Dominion, under the rule of the colonists, they would be doomed to inevitable degradation. Under such a rule as that which we maintain in India they will have a chance of rising, if it be in them to rise. The Kafirs have long taught us to respect and fear them as a brave and honourable tribe. The Zulus have earned a higher distinction : they have defeated an English General in the open field. They will multiply—either to be our credit or to be our shame. War among themselves kept their numbers down. When they can no longer fight, they will increase as the Irish increased. If we can succeed in educating them, no more honourable achievement will have to be recorded by the future historian of the British Empire. If we fail, we fail: but we shall have failed in an enterprise which even to have attempted will in some way redeem the stain of our dark and discreditable conquests.

The Transvaal, in spite of prejudices about the British flag, I still hope that we shall restore to its lawful owners.

LONDON : PRINTED BY
SPOTTISWOODE AND CO., NEW-STREET SQUARE
AND PARLIAMENT STREET

www.ingramcontent.com/pod-product-compliance
Lightning Source LLC
Chambersburg PA
CBHW021424090426
42742CB00009B/1244